The Nature Kid's Guide to
CHIPMUNKS

DAVID ANDERSON

LP Media Inc. Publishing
Text copyright © 2026 by LP Media Inc.
All rights reserved.

For information address LP Media Inc. Publishing,
30012 Variolite St NW, Princeton MN 55371
www.lpmedia.org

Publication Data

Chipmunks
The Nature Kid's Guide to Chipmunks — First edition.

Summary: "Learn all about Chipmunks, the Nature Kid Way"
— Provided by publisher.

ISBN: 979-8-89818-245-8

[1. Chipmunks – Non-Fiction] I. Title.

Title: The Nature Kid's Guide to Chipmunks

CONTENTS

FOREST FLOORS

Chipmunks keep their burrow entrance hidden with leaves and dirt. Some even dig fake entrances to trick predators!

Rustle! A tiny chipmunk stands on a rock and observes the forest.

Chipmunks are small animals that live on forest floors. They love woods with lots of trees and bushes. Fallen logs and rocks make great hiding spots for these quick little creatures.

Chipmunks dig **burrows** under the ground. A burrow is like a tiny house with rooms and tunnels. Some burrows stretch 30 feet long! The underground home keeps them safe and warm all year.

Eastern chipmunks live in forests across the eastern part of North America. Look near oak and maple trees. That is where they love to be!

HOME RANGE

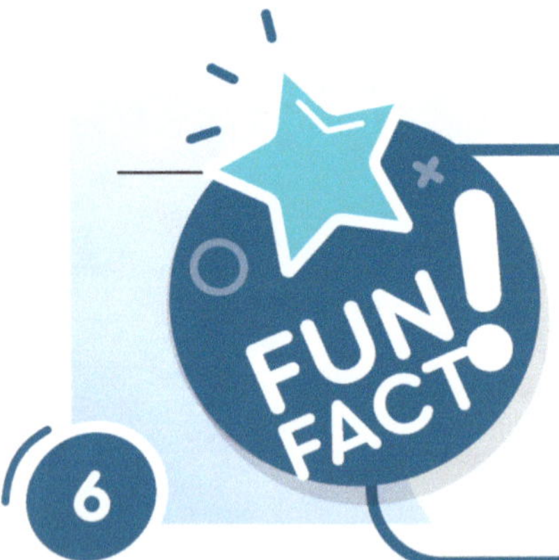

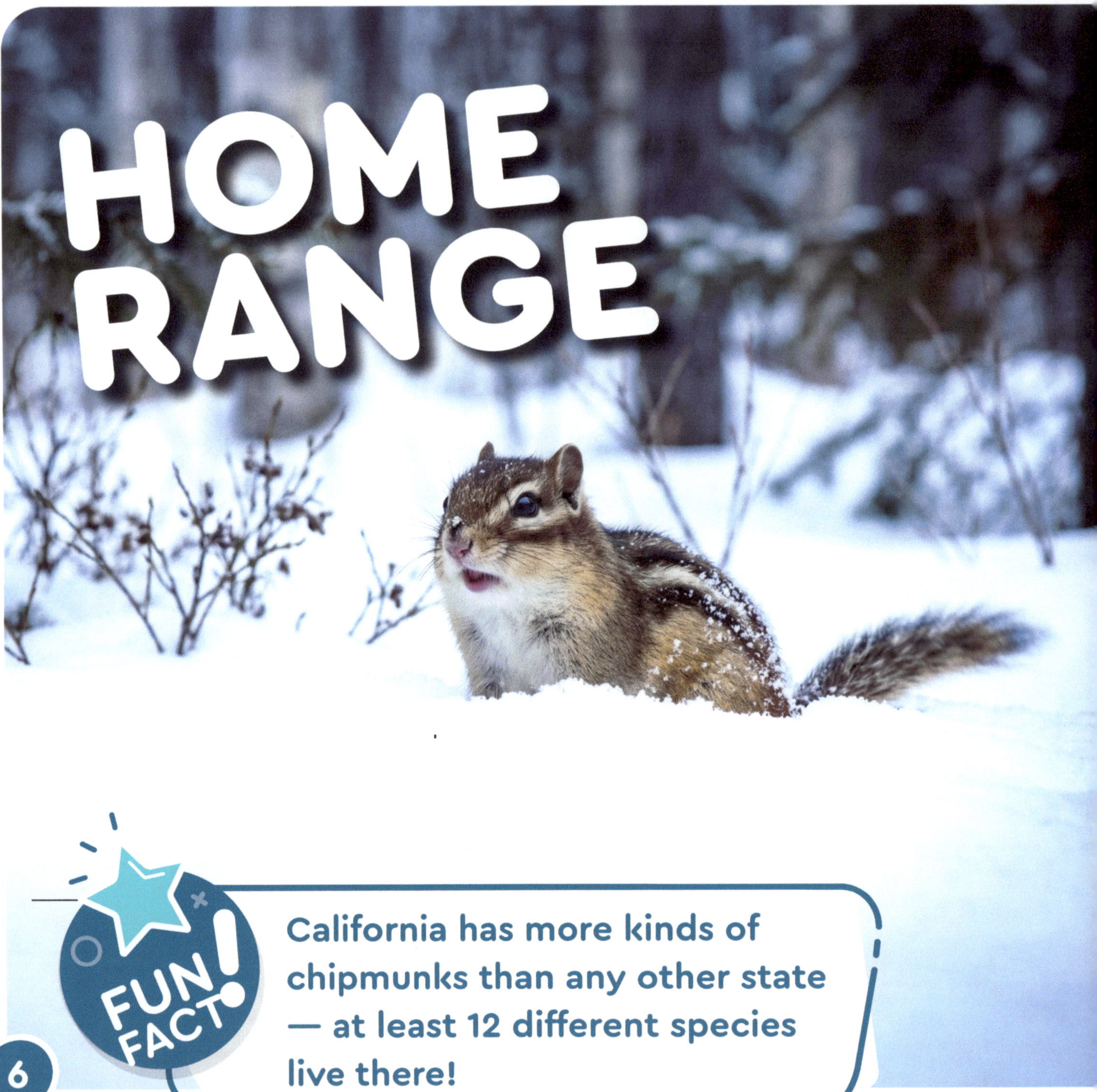

FUN FACT!

California has more kinds of chipmunks than any other state — at least 12 different species live there!

Chirp! A Siberian chipmunk calls out from a snowy Asian forest.

Most chipmunks live in North America. There are 25 different kinds in the world. You can find them from coast to coast, in forests, deserts, and mountains.

Some live in hot, dry deserts. Others live in cool, misty mountains. Chipmunks can make a home in many types of land because they adapt so well.

One special kind lives far away in Asia. The Siberian chipmunk lives in forests across Russia and China. It is the only kind found outside North America, making it truly unique.

TINY TOTS

A chipmunk's heart can beat around 350 times in just one minute — that is almost 6 beats every second!

Squeak! A tiny chipmunk pops out of a hole no bigger than your fist.

Chipmunks are tiny. Most are about 5 to 6 inches long, not counting their tail. They weigh only 1 to 5 ounces. Even the biggest ones would fit in your hand!

The least chipmunk is the smallest kind. It is not much bigger than a mouse. Its body is only about 4 inches long, and it weighs less than two nickels.

The eastern chipmunk is the largest type. It grows about 10 inches long with its tail. That is a bit shorter than a ruler, but it is a giant compared to its tiny cousins.

STRIPED STARS
DID YOU KNOW?
Chipmunks have four toes on their front feet and five on the back — perfect for gripping branches and digging tunnels.

Flash! Light and dark stripes blur as a Townsend's chipmunk runs.

Chipmunks have five dark stripes down their backs. Light stripes run between the dark ones. This bold pattern makes them easy to spot — and helps them hide in the forest shadows.

Big round eyes sit on the sides of their head. This lets them see almost all around without turning. Small rounded ears stick up on top, and sharp claws help them grip bark and dig in dirt.

Townsend's chipmunks have darker, thicker fur than most kinds. They live in the rainy forests of the Pacific Northwest. Their bushy tails help them balance as they climb high into the trees.

SUPER SENSES

Chipmunks use their whiskers to feel the width of tight spaces — if the whiskers fit, the chipmunk fits!

Snap! A chipmunk's ears twitch at a faraway sound in the woods.

Chipmunks have amazing senses. Their big eyes can see in almost every direction at once. This helps them spot danger quickly, whether it comes from above or below.

Sharp ears pick up tiny sounds. A chipmunk can hear a twig snap from far away. It freezes and listens carefully before it moves again.

Chipmunks also have a strong sense of smell. They use their noses to sniff out seeds buried underground. This skill helps them find food even under a blanket of snow.

HIDE WELL

Chipmunks sometimes flick their tails to confuse predators — the movement draws attention away from their body!
DID YOU KNOW?

Shh! A chipmunk freezes and blends into the brown leaves.

A chipmunk's stripes do more than look cool. They help it hide! The brown and tan colors match the forest floor perfectly.

When a chipmunk stays still, it is very hard to see. The stripes break up the shape of its body, making it look like shadows and sticks. A hawk flying above may not spot it at all.

Alpine chipmunks hide among rocks on tall mountains. Their gray and brown fur looks just like stone. Staying perfectly still is their best trick to stay safe from hungry predators.

NUTTY NIBBLES

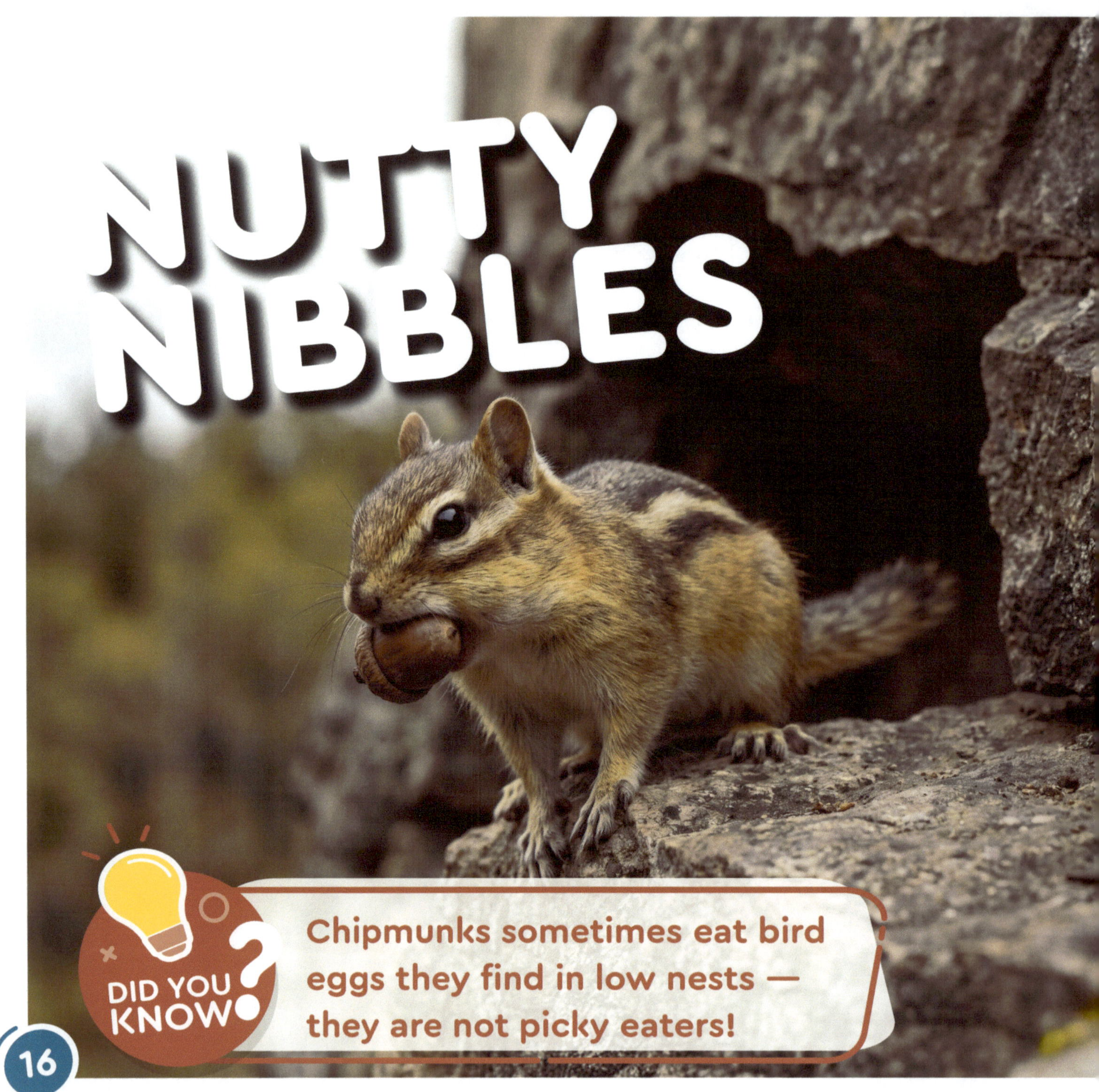

Crunch! A chipmunk bites into a big acorn on a rock.

Chipmunks eat many kinds of food. Nuts and seeds are their favorites. They also munch on berries, small fruits, and flower bulbs.

But chipmunks do not just eat plants. They catch bugs like beetles and caterpillars too. Sometimes they nibble on mushrooms or snack on snails. They eat whatever they can find!

Colorado chipmunks love the seeds of pine trees. In fall, they eat as much as they can. All that food gives them energy for the cold months ahead.

CHEEK STUFFERS

A chipmunk's cheek pouches can stretch to three times the size of its head!

18

Pop! Two acorns disappear into a chipmunk's puffy cheeks.

Chipmunks have stretchy pouches in their cheeks. They use them like grocery bags! A chipmunk fills its cheeks with seeds and nuts until they bulge out wide.

Once the pouches are full, it runs back to its burrow. It pushes the food out with its front paws. Then it goes right back for more, making trip after trip.

Cliff chipmunks gather food from rocky ledges and canyon walls. They stuff their cheeks and carry food to cracks in the rocks. Each trip brings more food closer to their hidden storage spots.

WATCH OUT

A chipmunk stops to look around for danger about every ten seconds — that is 360 safety checks every hour!

Screech! A hawk swoops down toward a chipmunk below.

Many animals hunt chipmunks. Hawks, owls, and eagles attack from the sky. Chipmunks must always watch above for shadows and swooping wings.

On the ground, foxes and weasels chase them. Snakes can slide right into burrows to find them. Even house cats catch chipmunks sometimes.

Red-tailed chipmunks live in mountain forests where they must watch for bobcats and coyotes too. With so many predators around, life is full of danger for these little animals.

DASH AWAY

FUN FACT!
A chipmunk burrow may have up to five different escape holes — like a house with five back doors!

Zip! A chipmunk vanishes into a crack between two rocks.

When danger is near, a chipmunk acts fast. It lets out a loud alarm call to warn others. Nearby chipmunks hear it and run for cover.

Then it dashes to its burrow or the nearest hiding spot. Chipmunks run in zigzag paths to confuse predators. They are quick, clever, and very hard to catch.

What makes them even harder to catch is how well they know their home range. Every rock, root, and burrow entrance is memorized. When it counts, that mental map saves their life.

ZIP ZOOM

DID YOU KNOW?

A chipmunk can sprint up to 15 miles per hour — that is faster than you can run!

Whoosh! A chipmunk leaps from one branch to the next.

Chipmunks are always on the move. They run, jump, and climb all day long. Their small, light bodies make them incredibly fast and nimble.

On the ground, they zip through grass and over rocks. Up in trees, they race along branches and leap across gaps. Their strong back legs push them forward with each big jump.

Some chipmunks live near rocky cliffs and steep hillsides. They hop from ledge to ledge with ease, never missing a step. Even the most uneven ground does not slow these little acrobats down.

BUSY DAYS

DID YOU KNOW?
Chipmunks spend about 15 hours a day inside their burrow — they only come out for about 9 hours!

Scratch! A chipmunk grooms its soft fur in the early morning sun.

Chipmunks wake up early. They are most active in the morning and late afternoon. The middle of the day? That is for resting in the cool burrow.

A chipmunk spends much of its time gathering food. It also **grooms** its fur, digs tunnels, and checks for danger. On warm days, it may sit on a sunny rock and soak up the heat.

This daily pattern repeats almost every single day through spring, summer, and fall. Each morning brings a new round of foraging, and each afternoon ends the same way — safely underground.

SOLO SQUAD

FUN
FACT!
Chipmunks that live near each other
learn to recognize each other's voice —
they know who is who by sound alone!

Chip! A long-eared chipmunk barks a warning to keep others away.

Chipmunks like to live alone. Each one has its own **home range** to protect. They do not share their space with other chipmunks — not even family.

If another chipmunk gets too close, there may be a chase. One chipmunk runs at the other to scare it off. They chatter loudly and stomp their tiny feet.

Long-eared chipmunks guard the land around their burrow fiercely. Each one watches over its own space in mountain forests. Neighbors learn quickly to stay on their own side of the invisible line.

CHIP CHATS

FUN FACT!

Some chipmunks mate twice a year — once in early spring and again in midsummer!

Trill! A Hopi chipmunk sings a special call to find a mate.

In spring, chipmunks are ready to mate. Males make soft chirping sounds to get attention. Females listen carefully and choose the best mate.

A male will chase a female through the woods. Sometimes many males chase one female at once! The fastest and strongest one usually wins.

Hopi chipmunks mate in the rocky canyons of the Southwest. After mating, the male leaves right away. The female takes care of everything on her own from that point forward.

CUTE KITS

DID YOU KNOW?
Chipmunk kits are born without any teeth but grow a full set within just a few weeks!

Peep! Two young chipmunks play outside their burrow.

Baby chipmunks are called **kits**. They are born with no fur, and their eyes are shut tight. A mother may have three to five kits at once, sometimes more.

Kits are incredibly tiny at birth — about the size of a jelly bean. They cannot see or hear for many weeks. The mother keeps them warm and safe deep in her burrow.

After about four weeks, kits begin to open their eyes for the first time. A few weeks after that, they are ready to poke their heads above ground and see the world.

MOM KNOWS

DID YOU KNOW?
Baby chipmunks first leave the burrow when they are about six weeks old!

Swish! A mother chipmunk carries her baby to a warm, safe spot.

Mother chipmunks do all the parenting. The father plays no part at all. She feeds and protects her kits completely by herself.

For the first few weeks, the babies drink their mother's milk. She stays close and keeps them warm. If danger comes near, she picks them up in her mouth and moves them to a safer spot.

After about two months the kits are ready to leave the burrow for good. Each one heads out alone to find its own home range and start life on its own.

SMART STASH

A single chipmunk may store over 8 pounds of food for winter — that is like you storing 500 pounds of snacks!

Thud! An acorn drops into a chipmunk's secret storage room.

Chipmunks are great planners. All fall long, they collect seeds and nuts. They hide food in many different spots underground, creating a secret pantry.

In winter, chipmunks go into a deep sleep called **torpor**. Their body slows way down to save energy. Every few days, they wake up, eat some stored food, and go back to sleep.

Some chipmunks store extra food in special burrow rooms. When spring finally comes, they wake up for good. Their secret stash kept them alive through the long, cold winter.

SPOT THEM

The name chipmunk may come from the sound of their loud chip call — they named themselves!

Skitter! A chipmunk dashes across a trail right in front of you.

Want to see a chipmunk? Head to a park or forest trail. Look near rocks, logs, and old stone walls. Morning is the best time to look.

Sit still and be quiet. Chipmunks are shy but curious. If you wait patiently, one may come close to check you out. Watch and enjoy, but do not chase or touch them.

Listen for a sharp, repeating chip chip chip call echoing through the trees. That sound means a chipmunk is nearby. Follow it quietly and you just might find a new furry friend!

GLOSSARY

burrow

A tunnel or hole dug underground where an animal lives.

groom

To clean and take care of fur.

home range

The area where one animal lives and finds its food.

kits

The name for baby chipmunks.

torpor

A deep sleep-like state where an animal's body slows way down to save energy through cold months